CONTENTS

❧ Lake Classic Short Stories ❧

"The universe is made of stories, not atoms."

—Muriel Rukeyser

"The story's about you."

—Horace

Everyone loves a good story. It is hard to think of a friendlier introduction to classic literature. For one thing, short stories are *short*—quick to get into and easy to finish. Of all the literary forms, the short story is the least intimidating and the most approachable.

Great literature is an important part of our human heritage. In the belief that this heritage belongs to everyone, *Lake Classic Short Stories* are adapted for today's readers. Lengthy sentences and paragraphs are shortened. Archaic words are replaced. Modern punctuation and spellings are used. Many of the longer stories are abridged. In all the stories,

5

painstaking care has been taken to preserve the author's unique voice.

Lake Classic Short Stories have something for everyone. The hundreds of stories in the collection cover a broad terrain of themes, story types, and styles. Literary merit was a deciding factor in story selection. But no story was included unless it was as enjoyable as it was instructive. And special priority was given to stories that shine light on the human condition.

Each book in the *Lake Classic Short Stories* is devoted to the work of a single author. Little-known stories of merit are included with famous old favorites. Taken as a whole, the collected authors and stories make up a rich and diverse sampler of the story-teller's art.

Lake Classic Short Stories guarantee a great reading experience. Readers who look for common interests, concerns, and experiences are sure to find them. Readers who bring their own gifts of perception and appreciation to the stories will be doubly rewarded.

🌿 Selma Lagerlöf 🌿
(1858–1940)

About the Author

Selma Lagerlöf was born in Ämtervik, Sweden. She grew up on her father's manor estate, Mårbacka—a place where only old-time traditions were observed. This very strict early upbringing made a strong and lasting impression on her novels and stories.

Lagerlöf did not feel at home with the growing emphasis on "realism" in the 1880s. Her first book, *Gosta Berling's Saga,* was published in 1891 when she was 33 years old. These tales of life in rural Sweden are both moral and mystical. In this book, as in her other writings, she turned to the past for both inspiration and plot.

Lagerlöf wrote a school reader that became very popular in her home country. In *The Wonderful Adventures of Nils,* she described the magical flight of a small boy throughout Sweden.

Lagerlöf traveled to Egypt and Palestine in 1899. There she met a colony of peasants who had come to Jerusalem to live as the first Christians did. On her return, she spent time on a similar commune in Sweden. These experiences inspired her epic novel *Jerusalem,* which brought her world fame. In 1909 she was awarded the Nobel prize.

Lagerlöf was interested in myth and legend. But her major theme was the problem of evil. Nearly all of her work centered on the human struggle to combine happiness with goodness.

Strangely, Lagerlöf herself could never quite accept the marvels and mysteries she wrote about. Literary scholars have aptly described her as "the great seeker who never achieved—and never claimed to achieve—certainty."

The Outlaws

Can innocent intentions
have disastrous results?
The two outlaws in this
story have very different
ways of looking at life. The
young fisherman has no
idea that his help could be
so harmful.

THE OUTLAW WOULD CATCH THE HUNTERS' SPEARS AND
THROW THEM RIGHT BACK.

The Outlaws

A peasant had killed a monk and fled to the woods. With that he became an outlaw, and a price was set upon his head. In the deep woods he met another outlaw. This fellow was a young fisherman from one of the islands. He had been accused of stealing a fishing net. The two became friends.

They made a home in a cave. Every day they went fishing and cooked their food together. They made their own arrows for hunting and watched out for each other.

The peasant could never leave the

forest. His crime had been too terrible. But the fisherman's crime was not as bad. Every now and then, he would carry to the village the game that they had killed. He didn't go into the middle of the village, of course. Instead, he would go to a few houses that were on the edge of town. There he would trade the game for milk, butter, arrowheads, and clothing.

The cave that was their home cut down deep into the side of a mountain. The entrance was hidden by wide slabs of stone and some bushes. High up on the hill stood a giant pine tree. The chimney of their fireplace opened up into its roots. The smoke from their fire drew up through the heavy hanging branches. Then it faded unseen into the air.

At first they were hunted as wild animals are. Then the two outlaws would hide in their dark cave, panting in terror. They would listen breathlessly as the hunters passed on. They didn't move until the noise and shouting faded away over the mountains.

For one long day, the young fisherman lay still. But the murderer could stand it no longer. He dashed out into the open where he could see his enemy. When they saw him and started chasing him, he didn't care. A chase was more to his liking than lying in quiet terror. He ran before the men who were chasing him. He jumped over streams and slid down hills.

The man had remarkable strengths and skills. Now all of them came alive. His body was like a steel spring. His eyes and ears were extra sharp. He knew the meaning of every whisper in the trees. He could understand the warning in an upturned stone.

Every time he climbed up the side of a cliff, he did the same thing. First he would stop to look down on his pursuers. Then he would greet them with loud songs of scorn. When their spears sang above him in the air, he would catch them and throw them back. As he dashed madly through the bushes, something within him seemed to sing out a wild song full of joy.

A bare hilltop rose from the forest. All alone at the top stood a tall pine tree. In its high, thick branches, a hawk's nest rocked in the breeze. So bold had the outlaw become that one day he climbed to the nest while he was being chased. He sat there and twisted the necks of the young hawks as the hunt went on beneath him.

The old birds flew screaming about him. They angrily swooped past his face. They struck at his eyes with their beaks and beat at him with their powerful wings. They clawed great scratches in his weathered skin.

The outlaw fought with the hawks, laughing. He stood up in the nest as he lunged at the birds with his knife. In the joy of the battle, he lost all thought of danger.

Then he remembered that he was being chased. He quickly turned to look for his enemies. But by then, the hunt had gone off in another direction. Not one of the hunters had thought of raising his eyes to the clouds. If one had, he would have seen the outlaw hanging there, fighting the hawks.

When he saw that he was safe, the man trembled from head to foot. He grabbed for a branch with his shaking hands. He looked down and groaned in fear of a fall. Now he felt afraid of the birds, afraid of being seen, and weakened by terror. Carefully and quickly, he slid back down the tree trunk. He lay down flat on the earth and crawled into the bushes. There he hid, weak and helpless, on the soft damp moss. A lone hunter could easily have captured him.

* * *

Tord was the name of the fisherman. He was only 16 years old, but he was strong and brave. By now he had lived for a whole year in the woods.

The peasant's name was Berg, but he was often called "The Giant." He was handsome and well-built—the tallest and strongest man in the entire county. The Giant had broad shoulders and yet was slender. His hands looked as if they had never known hard work. His hair was long and brown, and his face was a soft, light color.

By the time he had lived for a year in the forest, his look of strength had become awe-inspiring. Now he had bushy eyebrows and great muscles on his forehead. His lips were more firmly set than before. His strong cheekbones stood out more plainly. All the softer curves of his body had disappeared. His muscles had grown as strong as steel and his hair had turned salt-and-pepper gray.

Tord had never seen anyone so strong and mighty in all his life. In Tord's imagination, Berg was as tall as the forest and as strong as the raging surf. He served him as he would have served a master. He honored him as he would have honored a god.

It seemed quite natural that Tord should carry the hunting spear and drag the game home. It was also Tord's job to get the water and build the fire. Berg, the Giant, accepted all these services. But he never gave the boy a friendly word. The Giant looked upon the boy with contempt, as a common thief.

The outlaws did not live by stealing. Instead, they supported themselves by hunting and fishing. If Berg had not killed a holy man, the peasants would not have tried so hard to catch him. They would have just let him live in the mountains. But they feared a terrible disaster if they let Berg go unpunished.

When Tord took his game down into the valley, the peasants would tempt him with money and a pardon for himself. In trade, they wanted Tord to lead them to the cave of the Giant. They wanted to catch Berg in his sleep. But the boy always said no. If the peasants followed him, he would go the wrong way until they gave up.

Once Berg asked him about the peasants. He wanted to know if they had ever tried to get him to lead them to the cave. Tord told him the truth. Berg was surprised when he learned what reward they had offered. He said that Tord was a fool not to do it. Tord looked at him with something strange in his eyes. It was a look that Berg had never seen before. Not even in the eyes of his children or of his wife had he ever seen such love.

"You are my god, the ruler I have chosen of my own free will." This was what the eyes said. "You may scorn me or beat me if you like. But I shall still remain faithful to you."

From that moment, Berg paid more attention to the boy. He could see that Tord was brave in action but shy in speech. Death seemed to have no terrors for him. He would walk on the fresh ice of the mountain pools. He seemed to delight in danger.

To Tord, these daring feats made up for the wild ocean storms he could no longer go out to meet. But the night darkness of the woods still made him tremble. Even by day, the darkness of the forest shadows could frighten him. When Berg asked him about this, the boy was silent in shame.

Tord did not sleep in the bed at the back of the cave. Instead, after Berg was asleep, the boy would quietly creep to the entrance. There he would lie on one of the broad stones.

One day Berg found out about this. Even though he guessed the reason, he asked the boy about it. Tord would not answer. To avoid more questions, Tord slept in his bed for two nights. But then he went back to his post at the door.

One night, a snowstorm raged in the forest. When Tord woke in the morning, he found himself wrapped in a blanket of melting snow. A day or two later he fell ill. Sharp pains pierced his lungs when he tried to draw a breath. One evening, he fell down and could not rise to his feet again.

Berg came to his side and told him to rest in the warm bed. Tord groaned in agony, but he could not move. Berg put his huge arm under the boy's body and carried him to the bed.

The Giant had a strange feeling while he was helping the boy. It was as if he were touching a clammy snake. He had a taste in his mouth as if he had eaten bad meat. That was how terrible it made him feel to touch the person of a lowly common thief!

But Berg covered the sick boy with his own warm bearskin rug. He gave him some water. This was all he could do. Fortunately, the illness was not too dangerous, and Tord got well quickly. By then, Berg had done Tord's work and had taken care of him for a few days. Because of this, the two outlaws seemed to have become closer.

One day Tord dared to speak to Berg as they sat by the fire cutting their arrows.

"You come of good people, Berg," Tord said to his friend. "They are the richest peasants in the valley. The men in your family have served kings and fought in their castles."

"They have more often fought with the rebels," Berg answered.

"I have heard that your forefathers had

great feasts at Christmas time. And you had feasts, too—when you were at home. It is said that hundreds of men and women could find a place on the benches in your great hall.

"People say that hall was built in the days before St. Olaf came here. Great silver urns were there. Mighty horns filled with mead went the rounds of your table."

Berg sat on the edge of the bed. His head was in his hands. Now he pushed back the heavy hair that hung over his eyes. He smiled to himself at the pictures called up in his mind by Tord's words. Pictures of the great hall and of the silver urns danced before his eyes. He saw the richly dressed guests. He saw himself— Berg, the Giant—sitting in the place of honor. Yet he knew that even in the days of his glory, no one had ever looked at him with such pure admiration. Strangely, he was touched—and yet not pleased. He felt that this common thief had no right to admire him.

"Were there no feasts in your home?" he asked the young fisherman.

Tord laughed. "Out there on the rocks where Father and Mother live? Father steals from the shipwrecks, and Mother is a witch. When the weather is stormy, she rides out to meet the ships on a seal's back. Those who are washed overboard belong to her."

"What does she do with them?" asked Berg.

"Oh, a witch always needs dead bodies. She makes lotions from them, or perhaps she eats them. On moonlit nights, she sits out in the wildest surf. She looks for the little eyes and fingers of drowned children."

"That is horrible!" said Berg.

The boy answered calmly, "It would be for others—but not for a witch. She can't help it."

This was a new way of looking at life for Berg. "Then thieves *have* to steal, as witches have to make magic?" he asked.

"Why, yes, they do," answered the boy. "Everyone has to do the thing he was born for." Then a sly smile curled his lips. "But there are thieves who have never stolen," he added.

"What do you mean by that?" asked Berg with a frown.

The boy still smiled his sly smile. He seemed happy to have given Berg a riddle. "There are birds that do not fly. And there are thieves who have not stolen."

"How can anyone be called a thief if he hasn't ever stolen?" asked Berg.

The boy's lips closed tight as if to hold back the words. "But if one has a father who steals—" he said at last.

"A man may inherit house and money. But the name of thief is given only to the man who earns it," said Berg.

Tord laughed gently. "Oh? What if a mother begs her son to take the blame for the father's crime? The son might laugh at the hangman and run away into the woods. Do you see? A man may be called an outlaw for the sake of a fish net he has never seen."

Berg beat his fist on the stone table. He felt great anger. Here this strong, beautiful boy had thrown away his whole life for another! Neither love, nor riches, nor the respect of others could ever be his again. The struggle for food and clothing was all that was left to him in life. Berg had hated an innocent man—and this fool had let him do it! He scolded Tord. But Tord was not frightened any more than a sick child is frightened by the scolding of his worried mother.

* * *

High up on one of the wooded hills was a black swampy lake. It was square in shape, and its banks were straight. Its

corners were as sharp as if they had been
made by human hands. On three sides,
steep walls of rock rose up. Mountain
pines held on to the stones. Their roots
were as thick as a man's arm. At the
surface of the lake, these roots twisted
and coiled. They looked like snakes that
had been turned to stone.

Or did the twisted roots look more like
the skeletons of long-drowned giants?
The arms and legs were twisted in
strange positions. The long fingers
grasped deep into the rocks. The mighty
ribs were like arches holding the ancient
trees up. But now and again these steel
fingers would loosen their hold. Then the
strong north wind would throw a tree
from the ridge. Far out into the swamp
it would go. And there it would lie, its
crown deep in the muddy water. The
fishes found good hiding places around
its twigs. The roots rose out of the water
like the arms of some hideous monster.
They gave the lake a scary look.

The mountains sloped down on the fourth side of the little lake. A tiny stream turned among the rocks, forming a whole set of islands. Some of these islands were hardly big enough for a foothold. Others carried as many as 20 trees on their back.

Here, where the rocks were not high enough to shut out the sun, many trees grew. There were shy, gray-green alders, and leafy willows. Birches were there, too, and so were mountain ash and elder bushes. All of these beautiful trees gave the place great charm and fragrance.

By the lake, there was a forest of rushes as high as a man's head. The golden sunlight turned green as it fell upon the water. There were little clearings among the reeds. In the small ponds there, water-lilies slept under the watch of the tall rushes.

On a sunny day the outlaws came to one of these little ponds to fish. They waded through the reeds toward two high stones. There they sat, throwing out their bait for the big gleaming fish that slept just below the surface.

The outlaws' lives were now passed entirely among the mountains and the woods. Now they lived by the patterns of nature, just as the plants and animals do. When the sun shone, they were happy and merry. In the evening, they grew silent. The night, which had become very powerful, robbed them of their strength. Today the green light shining through the reeds put them into a magical mood.

Here they were completely shut off from the outer world. The reeds swayed gently in the soft wind. The rushes murmured. The long, ribbon-like leaves struck them lightly in the face. The two men sat quietly on the gray stones in their gray leather clothes. As much as humans could, they blended in with nature.

Each man sat across from the other,

as still as a stone statue. Among the reeds they saw giant fish glittering in all colors of the rainbow. When the men threw out their lines, they watched the rings on the water. It seemed to them that it was not they who had caused the widening rings to grow. A Nixie—half human, half fish—lay sleeping down in the water. She lay on her back. It was her breath that stirred the surface.

The green light seemed to shine through their eyes and into their brains. There they saw visions among the reeds—visions which they would not even tell to each other. There was not much fishing done. The day was given up to dreams and visions.

Then the sound of oars came from among the reeds. The men started up out of their dreaming. They saw a heavy boat, carved out of a tree trunk, coming toward them. The oars were not much wider than walking sticks.

Sitting in the boat was a young girl who had been gathering water-lilies. She had long, dark brown braids and great dark eyes. But she was strangely pale. Her cheeks were no darker than the rest of her face. Even her lips were pale. The girl wore a shirt of white linen and a leather belt with a golden clasp. Her skirt was blue with a wide red hem.

She rowed past the outlaws without seeing them. They sat absolutely still. This was not for fear of being seen, but because they wanted to look at her. When she had gone, the stone statues became men again. They smiled at each other.

"She was as white as the water-lilies," said one. "And her eyes were as dark as the water back there under the roots of the pines."

The sight of the girl made them so happy that they felt like laughing. "Did you think she was beautiful?" asked the Giant.

"I do not know. She passed by too quickly. Perhaps she *was* beautiful!"

"You probably did not dare to look at her. Did you think she was the Nixie?"

And again they felt a strange desire to laugh and laugh as children do.

* * *

As a child, Tord had once seen a drowned man. He had found the body on the beach in broad daylight. The sight of it had not frightened him. But that night he had bad dreams. In his dream, he was looking out over the ocean. Every wave threw a dead body at his feet. He saw all the rocks and islands covered with the bodies of the drowned. Of course, these drowned were dead. They belonged to the sea. But strangely, they could move and speak. In his dream, they pointed at him with their white, stiff fingers.

And so it happened again. The girl he had seen in the reeds appeared to him in his dreams. He met her at the bottom of the lake. The light was even greener than in the reeds. There he had time enough to see that she was indeed beautiful.

Tord dreamed that he sat on one of the great pine roots in the middle of the lake. The tree rocked up and down—first under, then over, the surface of the water. At last he saw her on one of the smallest islands. She stood under the red mountain ash tree and laughed at him. His very last dream had been the best of all. In that dream, she had kissed him.

But then it was morning, and Tord heard Berg rising. He kept his eyes closed, hoping to go on with his dream. When he did awake, he was dazed from what he had seen during the night. All that day, he thought more and more about the girl. Toward evening, he asked Berg if he knew her name.

Berg looked at him sharply. "I suppose it is better for you to know it at once," he said. "The girl is called Unn. We are related to each other."

Somehow Tord knew that this girl was the cause of Berg's wild, hunted life. Now he tried to remember what he had heard about her.

Unn was the daughter of a free peasant. Because her mother was dead, she was in charge of her father's household. This was to her taste, for she was independent by nature. She had no wish to give herself to any husband. Unn and Berg were cousins. The rumor had gone about that Berg was attracted by the girl. Hour after hour he liked to sit talking with Unn and her maids. He would rather do that than work in his own house.

One Christmas a great feast was to be given in Berg's hall. His wife had invited a monk. She had hoped that this holy man would speak to Berg. She wanted the monk to show him how wrong it was to spend so much of his time with Unn.

Berg and other guests had no use for this monk. For one thing, they didn't like the way he looked. He was very fat and absolutely white. The ring of hair around his bald head was white. His eyebrows were white. The color of his skin and all his clothing was white. Many found him very ugly to look at.

But the monk was fearless. He thought that his words would mean more if many people heard them. He stood up at the table before all the guests. He said, "Why do men call the cuckoo the most evil of birds? Because he brings up his young in the nest of others. But here sits just such a man. He takes no care for his house and his children. No! He seeks his pleasure with a strange woman. I will call him the most evil of men."

Unn rose in her place. "Berg, this is said to you and to me!" she cried. "Never have I been so shamed. And my father is not here to protect me." Then she turned to go, and Berg hurried after her.

"Stay where you are," Unn said. "I do not wish to see you again." He stopped her by the door. He asked her what he could do to make her stay with him. Her eyes glowed. She answered that he himself should know best what had to be done. Then Berg went back into the hall and killed the monk.

For a while, Berg and Tord thought the same thoughts. Then Berg said, "You should have seen her when the white monk fell! My wife drew the children about her and cursed Unn. She turned the faces of the children toward her. She told them to remember this always. For this woman's sake, their father had become a murderer!

"But, as she stood there, Unn had never been so quiet and so beautiful! The men who saw her trembled. She thanked me for the deed. Then she told me to run to the woods at once. She told me never to become a thief, and to use my knife only in a just cause."

"Your deed had made her noble," said Tord with a smile.

And once again Berg found himself surprised by his companion. Tord was a heathen, or worse than a heathen. He never spoke against that which was wrong. He seemed to have no sense of the rules of society. In Tord's mind, what had to come, came. Only by name did he know God, Christ, and the saints. His mother was learned in magic. She had taught him to respect and fear the spirits of the dead.

Then it was that Berg began a foolish task. He might as well have woven a rope for his own neck! Berg decided to open the eyes of this ignorant boy to the power of God, the Lord of all Justice. He taught him all the things that mankind had learned to do to soften God's anger. He told him of pilgrims who traveled to holy places. He told him of holy monks who had given up the joys of the world.

The more he spoke, the paler the boy became. Berg would have stopped, but his thoughts carried him away. At last, night sank down upon them. In the black forest night, an owl screamed through the stillness.

* * *

When autumn came, a storm came along with it. Tord was out in the woods alone. He had gone there to check his many traps and snares. Berg had stayed behind to mend his clothes. The boy's path led him up a wooded hill. As he walked, the falling leaves danced in circles around his feet.

Again and again he had the feeling that someone was walking behind him. He turned around several times. Then he saw it was only the wind and went on again. But he had not silenced the sounds of his vision. At first he thought he heard the tiny dancing feet of elfin children. Then he thought he heard the hissing of a great snake moving up behind him. Beside the snake there came a wolf. It seemed to Tord that the tall, gray creature was waiting for the snake to strike. Then it would surely spring upon his back.

Tord started to walk faster, but the visions speeded up with him. When the creatures seemed only two steps behind him, he turned. But nothing was there, as he had known all the time. He sat down upon a stone to rest. It seemed that the leaves of all the forest trees had fallen at his feet. He saw the little yellow birch leaves and the red mountain ash leaves. He also saw the dried, black-brown leaves of the elm. Scattered about were the bright red leaves of the aspen and the yellow-green leaves of the willows.

These leaves were all faded, broken, and scarred. On this cold fall day, they looked nothing like the tender green shoots that had unrolled from the buds in spring.

"You are sinners!" cried the boy. "All of us are sinners. Nothing is pure in the eyes of God. You have already been dried up in the flame of his anger."

Then he got up and walked on again. Beneath him the forest floor waved like a stormy sea. But he heard something that he had never heard before. Now the woods around him were full of voices. First it was like a whispering, and then like a gentle cry. Suddenly it became a loud threat and a roaring curse. Then it laughed and moaned. It was as the voice of hundreds. The voices almost drove him mad. He shivered in deadly terror. It was the same feeling he had when he lay in the cave, listening to his pursuers in the forest. Now he seemed to hear again the crashing of the branches. He heard the heavy footsteps of the men and their wild shouts.

The storm that roared about him was strange indeed. There was something else in it—something terrible. There were voices he could not understand, speaking in a strange language.

Tord had heard many storms that were mightier than this while out on his fishing boat. But he had never heard the wind playing on a harp of so many strings. Every tree seemed to have its own voice. Every hill and gully sang its own song. The loud echo from the rocky wall shouted back in still another voice. He knew all these sounds—yet now there was an even louder voice along with them. It was this strange voice that awoke a storm of voices within his own head and heart.

When he was alone, Tord had always been afraid in the darkness of the wood.

He loved the open sea and the cliffs. The woods were different. Ghosts and spirits hid there in the shadows of the trees.

Then suddenly Tord knew who was speaking to him in the storm. It was God—the Lord of all Justice! Surely God was chasing after him because of his friend. God wanted him to give up the murderer of the monk!

Tord began to speak aloud into the storm. He told God what he wanted to do. But he said that he could not do it. Tord said that he had wanted to speak to the Giant. He wanted to beg him to make his peace with God. But he could not find the words.

"I now know that the world is ruled by a God of Justice," Tord shouted into the wind. "Now I know that Berg is a lost man. I have wept through the night for my friend. I know that God will find him no matter where he may hide. But, because of my love for him, I cannot find the words to talk to him. Do not ask me to speak to him! Do not ask that the ocean shall rise up as high as the mountains."

He fell silent again. The deep voice of the storm, which he knew was God's voice, was silent also. The wind stopped suddenly. Then Tord saw a burst of sunshine. He heard a sound as of oars and the gentle movement of stiff reeds. These sounds brought back the memory of the girl Unn.

Then the storm began again. Now he heard steps behind him, and a harsh, breathless panting. This time, he did not dare to turn. He knew it was the white monk! Surely he had come from the feast in Berg's great hall, covered with blood. Tord knew that he had an open ax cut in his forehead. He could hear the monk whispering, "Betray him, Tord! Give him up, so that you may save his soul."

Tord began to run. He tried to run

away from his growing terror. But as he ran he heard the deep, mighty voice behind him. He knew it was the voice of God. He had no doubt that it was God himself chasing him—demanding that he give up the murderer.

Tord thought again about Berg's crime. Now it seemed more horrible to him than it had ever seemed before. An unarmed man had been murdered! A servant of God had been cut down with an ax. What greater sin could there be?

How could it be that the murderer still dared to live? After what he had done, how did he dare to enjoy the light of the sun and the fruits of the earth? Tord stopped, clenched his fists, and screamed a loud threat. Then, like a madman, he ran from the forest. He went down into the valley.

* * *

When Tord entered the cave, the outlaw was sitting on the stone bench, sewing. The fire gave off only a pale light, and Berg's work was not going well. The boy's heart swelled in true pity. This wonderful Giant seemed all at once so poor and so unhappy.

"What is the matter?" asked Berg. "Are you ill? Have you been frightened of something?"

Then for the first time Tord spoke of his fear. "It was so strange in the forest. Today I heard the voices of spirits and saw ghosts. I saw white monks."

"Boy!"

"They sang to me all the way up the hill. I ran from them, but they ran after me, singing. What do those ghosts want with me? There are others who need their presence more than I."

"Are you crazy tonight, Tord?" the Giant asked.

Now the boy spoke without knowing what words he was using. It seemed that his shyness had left him all at once.

"They were white monks," he insisted, "pale as dead bodies. And their clothes were spotted with blood. Their hoods were pulled down over their foreheads. But I could still see the wound shining there. I could see the great, yawning, red wound from the ax."

"Tord," said the Giant, growing pale and very serious. "The saints alone know why you see the mark of an ax. I killed the monk with a knife."

Tord stood trembling before Berg. He was wringing his hands. "They demand that I lead them to you. They want me to betray you."

"Who? The monks?"

"Yes, yes, the monks. They show me visions. They show me Unn. They show me the open, sunny ocean. They show me the camps of the fishermen, where there is dancing and joy. Even when I close my eyes, I can see it all. 'Leave me!' I say to them. 'My friend has killed a man—but he is not bad. Leave me alone, and I will talk to him. He will see the wrong he has done. He will make up for his crime.'"

"And what do the monks answer?" asked Berg. "I suppose they do not want to pardon me. No doubt they want to torture me and to burn me at the stake."

Tord went on. "'Shall I betray my best friend?' I ask them. 'He is all that I have in the world. He saved me from the bear when its claws were already at my throat. We have suffered hunger and cold together. He covered me with his own blankets while I was ill. I have brought him wood and water. I have watched over his sleep. I have led his enemies far from his trail.'

"Why should those ghosts think me a man who betrays his friend? My friend will go to the priest himself. He will confess to him. I will go with him. Together we will seek forgiveness."

Berg listened silently, his keen eyes

searching Tord's face. "Go to the priest yourself. Tell him the truth. You must go back again among people."

"What does it help if I go alone? Because of your sin, the spirits of the dead follow me. Do you not see how I tremble before you? You have lifted your hand against God himself! What crime is as bad as yours? Why did you tell me about the just God? It is you yourself who force me to betray you. Berg! Spare me this sin. Go to the priest yourself." He sank down on his knees before the Giant.

The murderer laid his hand on the boy's head and looked closely at him. Now he measured his sin by the fear of his friend. It grew and grew to a monstrous size. He saw himself in conflict with the will that rules the world. Sorrow for what he had done filled his heart.

"Woe unto me that I did what I did!" he cried. "Isn't this miserable life we lead in the forest punishment enough? Have I not lost my home and fortune? Have I not lost my friends, and all the joys that make the life of a man? What more?"

As he heard his friend speak this way, Tord jumped up in wild terror. "You can repent!" he cried. "Do my words move your heart? Oh, then come with me, come at once. Come, let us go while there is yet time."

Berg the Giant jumped up also. "You did it already?"

"Yes, yes, yes! I have betrayed you. But come quickly. Come now, now that you can repent. We must escape. We will escape."

The murderer stooped to the ground. The battle-ax of his fathers lay at his feet. "Son of a thief," he hissed. "I trusted you. I loved you."

When Tord saw him stoop for the ax, he knew that his own life was in danger. He tore his own ax from his belt, and thrust it at Berg before he could rise.

Then the Giant fell to the floor, his blood spurting out over the cave. In the mass of hair on Berg's forehead, Tord saw the great, yawning, red wound from the ax in his own hand.

At that moment, the peasants stormed into the cave. They praised Tord for what he had done. They told him that he would receive a full pardon.

Tord looked down at his hands. He could almost see the chains that had drawn him on to kill the man he loved. They were woven out of empty air. They were woven out of the green light in the reeds. They were woven out of the shadows in the woods and the song of the storm. They were woven out of the magic vision of dreams. And he said out loud, "God is great."

Tord bent down beside the body and spoke through his tears to the dead man. He begged him to awake. The villagers made a litter of their spears. On this litter they would carry the body of the free peasant back to his home. They felt awed by the dead man and softened their voices in his presence. When they lifted him up, Tord stood up too and shook the hair from his eyes. Then he spoke in a soft voice.

"Berg the Giant became a murderer for the sake of Unn. I, Tord the fisherman, whose father is a thief and whose mother is a witch, killed Berg. Go and tell Unn why Tord killed Berg. Tell her that Berg had taught him that justice is the cornerstone of the world."

Kevenhüller

Have you ever been given a gift "with strings attached"? In this story a talented inventor is rewarded with a magical gift. Why does Kevenhüller wish he could give it back?

"LOOK! KEVENHÜLLER IS GOING TO FLY!"

Kevenhüller

Kevenhüller was born in Germany in the year 1770. He was the son of a count. If he had wanted to, he could have lived in a beautiful palace and ridden at the Emperor's side. But he had not.

What he wished for was something quite different. He would have liked to fill the castle with whirling wheels and working levers. But when he could not do it, he left his easy life. He became an apprentice to a watchmaker. In that busy shop he learned everything there was to learn about cogwheels, springs, and pendulums. He learned to make sun-dials and star-dials. He learned to make clocks with singing birds and horn-blowing shepherds.

Kevenhüller made huge clocks with chimes that filled a whole church tower with their wonderful machinery. He made watches so small that they could be set inside a locket.

At last Kevenhüller had learned all he could from the watchmaker. He made up his mind to leave. One day he put his knapsack on his back, took his stick in his hand, and said good-bye. For a long time he wandered from place to place. He wanted to study everything that moved with lots of rollers and wheels. Kevenhüller was certainly no ordinary watchmaker. He wanted to be a great inventor and to improve the world.

After he had wandered through many lands, he turned his steps toward Värmland. There he wanted to study mill-wheels and mining. One beautiful summer morning, he was crossing the marketplace of Karlstad. It was a day like any other.

But that same morning, the wood nymph had decided to walk to the town. Now the noble lady was crossing the marketplace from the other direction. So she met Kevenhüller.

The wood nymph had shining green eyes and a mass of light hair. Her beautiful hair reached almost to the ground. She was dressed in a gown of strange green silk that kept changing colors. She was the most beautiful woman that Kevenhüller had ever seen.

For a moment he stood as if he had lost his wits. He stared at her as she came toward him.

She had come straight from the deepest part of the woods. They say the ferns there are as high as trees. The giant firs shut out the sun. The only light in these deep woods falls in golden drops on the yellow moss.

I would like to have been walking in Kevenhüller's place that day. I would like to have seen the ferns and pine needles tangled in her yellow hair. I heard that she also had a little black snake about her neck.

How the people stared at her! Horses bolted—frightened by her long, floating hair. The street boys ran after her. The working men dropped their meat axes to gape at her.

She herself was calm and queenly. She smiled only a little at all the excitement. Kevenhüller saw her small, pointed teeth shining between her red lips.

The wood nymph had hung a cloak over her shoulders so that no one could see who she was. But as bad luck would have it, she had forgotten to cover her tail! Now it dragged along the paving stones.

Kevenhüller saw the tail. He was sorry that a noble lady should be made fun of by the town. So he bowed to her politely.

"Would it not please your Grace to lift your train?" he asked.

The wood nymph was touched—not only by his kindness, but by his politeness. She stopped before him and looked at him. He had a strange feeling. It seemed to him that shining sparks passed from her eyes to his brain. "Kevenhüller," she said, "from now on, you shall be able to make anything you want. But you will be able to make only one of each kind."

He knew that she could keep her word. For who can doubt that the wood nymph has great power? Everyone knows that she can give genius and wonderful powers to those who win her favor.

Kevenhüller stayed in Karlstad and opened a large workshop there. He hammered and worked night and day. In a week he had made a wonder. It was a carriage which moved by its own power! All by itself, the wonderful carriage went uphill and downhill. It went fast or slow.

It could be steered and turned, stopped and started, as one wished.

Kevenhüller became famous. He was so proud of his carriage that he went to Stockholm. He wanted to show it to the king. To get there, he did not need to hire a horse or carriage. He proudly rode to Stockholm in his own carriage. In just a few hours, he rode right up to the palace. The king came out with the ladies and gentlemen of his court. They all looked at the carriage in wonder. They could not praise him enough.

The king then said, "You might give that carriage to me, Kevenhüller." And even though he answered no, the king insisted. He did not want to accept that answer.

Then Kevenhüller saw a fair-haired court lady wearing a green dress. He knew who she was. And somehow he also knew something else. It was she who had told the king to ask him for his carriage! He was in despair. He could not bear that anyone else should have his carriage. Yet how could he say no to the king? So Kevenhüller drove the carriage with great speed into the palace wall! It was broken into a thousand pieces.

When he came home to Karlstad, Kevenhüller tried to start work on another carriage. But he could not. Now he became upset at the gift the wood nymph had given him.

He had left behind the easy life at his father's castle to do great things for many people. It was never his idea to make wonders which only *one* person could use. What good was it to him to be a great master—even the greatest of all masters? His work was useless if he could not make copies for a thousand other people!

Kevenhüller longed for quiet, sensible work. He became a stone cutter and mason. It was then that he built the great stone tower by the west bridge. His idea was to go on building. Next he would add walls and courtyards, ramparts and turrets. In the end it would be a beautiful castle.

There, standing by the Klar River, he would have his childhood's dream. His castle would have room for everything that had to do with making things. Every kind of work would have a place in the castle halls. Millers and blacksmiths would have shops there. Watchmakers with green shades over their strained eyes would work there, too. There would be dyers with dark hands, and weavers, turners, filers. All would have their workshops in his castle.

At first everything went as he had planned. He built the tower of the stones he himself had cut. Then he put windmill sails on it—for the tower was to be a working mill. Now he wanted to begin on the blacksmith's shop.

But one day, he stood and watched the light, strong sails of his windmill. He thought about wings as he watched the sails turning in the wind. Then his old longing came over him.

He shut himself in in his workshop. He tasted no food, took no rest, and worked without stopping. At the end of a week, he had made a new marvel.

The next day he climbed up on the roof of his tower. He began to fasten the wings he had made to his shoulders.

Two boys playing on the street saw him. They gave a loud cry that was heard through the whole town. Then they ran off. Panting and puffing, they ran up the streets and down the streets. They knocked on all the doors, screaming as they ran. "Kevenhüller is going to fly! Kevenhüller is going to fly!"

The inventor stood calmly on the roof of the tower. He fastened on his wings. Meanwhile, crowds of people came running through the narrow streets of old Karlstad. Soon the bridge was crowded with them. The marketplace was packed. Even the banks of the river swarmed with people.

At last Kevenhüller got his wings on and set out. With just a couple of flaps, he was out in the air. Now he floated high above the earth.

Kevenhüller drew in the air with long breaths—it was strong and pure. His chest expanded, and the blood rushed through his veins. He tumbled like a pigeon. He hovered like a hawk. He flew as swift as the swallow. His flight was as sure as the falcon's.

If only he could make a pair of wings for every one of the people watching him! If only he could give them all the power to fly! Alas, he could not enjoy it alone. Ah, that wood nymph—if he could only meet her!

Then he saw something come flying toward him. He saw that the thing was flying with great wings like his own. He saw floating yellow hair, green silk, and wild shining eyes. It was she, it was she!

Kevenhüller did not stop to think. With furious speed he threw himself upon her. He wanted to kiss her or to strike her—he was not sure which. But more than anything, he wanted to force her to take back the power that she had given him.

It seemed that he did not look where he was going. He saw only the flying hair and the wild eyes. As he came up close to her, he stretched out his arms to grab her. But his wings caught in hers. Because hers were the stronger, his wings were torn and destroyed. In a moment he was swung around and thrown down—he knew not where.

When he came to, he was lying on the roof of his own tower. The broken wings were by his side. He had flown right into his own mill! The windmill sails had caught him and whirled him around a few times. Then they had thrown him down on the tower roof.

So that was the end.

Kevenhüller was again a desperate man. He could not bear the thought of ordinary work. Yet he did not dare to use his magic power. He knew what would happen if he made another wonder. In the end he would have to destroy it—and his heart would break. But if he did not destroy it, something terrible would happen. The thought that he could do no good for others with his gift was driving him mad.

Again he picked up his knapsack and his walking stick. He let the mill stand as it was. Out he went to search for the wood nymph.

Along the way, he came to Ekeby. This was a large community for retired people. He was well received there, and there he remained. The memories of his childhood came back to him. He allowed the people of Ekeby to call him count. Over time his hair grew gray and his brain slept. He became so old that he could no longer believe in the feats of his youth. He was not the man who could work wonders. It was not he who had made the self-moving carriage and the flying machine. Oh, no—tales, tales!

But then everything changed. Life there had never been worse. A storm passed over the land. Men went to war, and souls went to heaven. Wolves came from the woods with witches on their backs. And the wood nymph came to Ekeby.

No one in the town knew who she was. They thought that she was a poor woman who had a cruel mother-in-law. They thought she had been thrown out of her own home. So they gave her a place to stay. They honored her like a queen and loved her like a child.

Kevenhüller alone saw who she was. At first he was dazzled like the others. But one day she wore a dress of green silk. When she had that on, Kevenhüller recognized her.

There she sat on silk pillows. All the old men were serving her. One was a cook, and another was a footman. One was a reader, and another played music for her. One made her shoes. They all had their jobs.

They said that they were caring for her because she was ill. But Kevenhüller knew better than that. She was laughing at them all.

He tried to warn the townspeople against her. "Just look at her small, pointed teeth," he said. "Look at her wild, shining eyes. *She is the wood nymph.* All evil is about in these terrible times. I tell you she is the wood nymph, come here to ruin us. I have seen her before."

But a strange thing happened to Kevenhüller after he saw the wood nymph. Suddenly he had the strong desire to work again. This desire began to burn in his brain. His fingers ached with longing to bend themselves around some tools. He could wait no longer. With a bitter heart, he put on his work clothes. Then he shut himself up in a workshop.

A cry went out from Ekeby over the whole of Värmland. "Kevenhüller has begun to work!"

A new wonder would soon see the light. What should it be? Will he teach us to walk on the water? Will he make a ladder to reach to the stars?

One night, the first or second of October, Kevenhüller had the wonder ready. He came out of the workshop carrying it in his hand. It was a wheel that turned without stopping. As it turned, the spokes glowed like fire, giving out lots of warmth and light. Kevenhüller had made a sun! When he came out of the workshop with it, the night grew bright. Sparrows began to chirp and the clouds began to burn as if it were dawn.

Kevenhüller was amazed at his own work. There should never again be darkness or cold on earth! His head whirled when he thought of it. The sun would continue to rise and set. But when it went down, thousands and thousands of his fire-wheels would flame through the land.

Even in December, the air would be as warm as it is on the hottest summer day. Harvests would ripen in the winter. Wild strawberries would cover the hills the whole year round. Ice would never form on the water.

His fire-wheel would create a new world. It would be warm furs to the poor and bright sun to the miners. It would give power to the mills and life to nature. It would give a new, rich, and happy life to all people.

But at the same time, Kevenhüller knew that it was all a dream. The wood nymph would never let him make another wheel. Again he felt great anger and a longing for revenge. He thought that he would kill her. After that he no longer knew what he was doing.

Kevenhüller went to the main building of Ekeby. In the hall under the stairs, he put down his fire wheel. It was his plan to set fire to the house—and burn up the wood nymph in it!

Then he went back to his workshop. For a while he sat there, just silently listening. There was shouting and crying outside. Now the people of Ekeby could see that a great deed was done.

Yes, run, scream, ring the alarm! Kevenhüller thought to himself. But she is burning in there—the wood nymph whom you sat on silk pillows!

May she suffer long! May she run before the flames from room to room! Ah, how the green silk will blaze! How the flames will play in her hair. Courage, flames! Courage! Catch her. Set fire to her. Witches burn! Fear not her magic, flames! Let her burn! There is one who for her sake must burn his whole life through.

Soon bells rang and wagons came

rattling. Pumps were brought out and water was carried up from the lake. People came running from all the neighboring villages. There were cries and wailings and commands. That was the roof, which had fallen in. There was the terrible crackling and roaring of a fire. But still, none of this disturbed Kevenhüller. He sat on the chopping block and rubbed his hands.

Finally he heard a crash, as if the heavens had fallen. He started up in triumph. "Now it is done!" he cried. "Now she cannot escape. Now she is crushed by the beams or burned up by the flames. At last it is done."

Then Kevenhüller thought of the honor and glory of Ekeby. It had all been sacrificed to get her out of the world! The beautiful halls—which had held so much happiness—could never be replaced. Nor could the tables, the precious old furniture, or the silver and china.

Now he jumped up with a cry. His firewheel—had he not put it under the stairs to cause the fire?

Kevenhüller looked down on himself. He was so upset that he could hardly move a muscle.

"Am I going mad?" he said. "How could I do such a thing?"

At the same moment, the door of the workshop opened. The wood nymph walked in.

Smiling and fair, she stood at the door. Her green dress had neither hole nor stain. No smoke darkened her yellow hair. She was just as he had first seen her in the marketplace so long ago. Again her tail hung between her feet. All of the wildness and sweet fragrance of the wood was about her.

"Ekeby is burning," she said with a laugh.

Kevenhüller lifted a sledgehammer. He meant to throw it at her head. But then he saw that she had his fire-wheel in her hand.

"See what I have saved for you," she said to him.

Kevenhüller threw himself on his knees before her.

"You have broken my carriage. You have torn my wings. And you have ruined my life. Have pity on me!"

She climbed up on the bench and sat there. Strangely, she was just as young and mischievous now as when he first saw her.

"I see that you know who I am," she said.

"I know you. I have always known you," said the unfortunate man. "You are genius. But set me free! Take back your gift! Let me be an ordinary person! Why do you hurt me? Why do you destroy me?"

"Madman!" cried the wood nymph. "I have never wished you any harm. I gave you a great reward. But I can also take it away from you if you wish. Yet think about this well! *You will be sorry about it if I do.*"

"No, no!" he cried. "Take it away! I do not want the power of working wonders!"

"First, you must destroy this," she said. She threw the fire-wheel on the ground in front of him.

Kevenhüller did not hesitate. He swung the sledgehammer over the shining sun. Sparks flew about the room. Splinters and flames danced about him. His last wonder lay about him in pieces.

"Yes—now I take my gift from you," said the wood nymph. As she stood in the door, he looked at her for the last time. She was more beautiful than ever. No longer did she seem evil, but only stern and proud.

"Madman!" she cried again. "Did I ever forbid you to let *others* copy your works? I only wished to protect the man of genius from a mechanic's labor."

Then she left. Kevenhüller really did become a madman for a couple of days. Then he was himself again.

But in his madness he had burned down the main house of Ekeby! No one was hurt. Still, it was a great sorrow to the retired people who lived there. They had enjoyed many good things in that fine, big house. It was sad that they should have to lose it.

Thinking About
the Stories

The Outlaws

1. Compare and contrast at least two characters in this story. In what ways are they alike? In what ways are they different?

2. Did the story plot change direction at any point? Explain the turning point of the story.

3. Where does this story take place? Is there anything unusual about it? What effect does the place have on the characters?

Kevenhüller

1. Who is the main character in this story? Who are one or two of the minor characters? Describe each of these characters in one or two sentences.

2. Does the main character in this story have an internal conflict? Does a terrible decision have to be made? Explain the character's choices.

3. The plot is the series of events that takes place in a story. Usually, story events are linked in some way. Can you name an event in this story that was the cause of a later event?

Thinking About
the Book

1. Choose your favorite illustration in this book. Use this picture as a springboard to write a new story. Give the characters different names. Begin your story with something they are saying or thinking.

2. Compare the stories in this book. Which was the most interesting? Why? In what ways were they alike? In what ways different?

3. Good writers usually write about what they know best. If you wrote a story, what kind of characters would you create? What would be the setting?

LAKE CLASSICS

Great American Short Stories I

Washington Irving, Nathaniel Hawthorne, Mark Twain, Bret Harte, Edgar Allan Poe, Kate Chopin, Willa Cather, Sarah Orne Jewett, Sherwood Anderson, Charles W. Chesnutt

Great American Short Stories II

Herman Melville, Stephen Crane, Ambrose Bierce, Jack London, Edith Wharton, Charlotte Perkins Gilman, Frank R. Stockton, Hamlin Garland, O. Henry, Richard Harding Davis

Great British and Irish Short Stories I

Arthur Conan Doyle, Saki (H. H. Munro), Rudyard Kipling, Katherine Mansfield, Thomas Hardy, E. M. Forster, Robert Louis Stevenson, H. G. Wells, John Galsworthy, James Joyce

Great Short Stories from Around the World I

Guy de Maupassant, Anton Chekhov, Leo Tolstoy, Selma Lagerlöf, Alphonse Daudet, Mori Ogwai, Leopoldo Alas, Rabindranath Tagore, Fyodor Dostoevsky, Honoré de Balzac

Cover and Text Designer: Diann Abbott

Library of Congress Catalog Number: 94-075343
ISBN 1-56103-042-2
Printed in the United States of America
1 9 8 7 6 5 4 3 2

LAKE CLASSICS

Great Short Stories
from Around the World I

Selma
LAGERLÖF

Stories retold by Emily Hutchinson
Illustrated by James McConnell

LAKE EDUCATION
Belmont, California